Celebrating
Thanksgiving

By: Shelly Nielsen

Illustrated by: Marie-Claude Monchaux

Published by Abdo & Daughters, 6535 Cecilia Circle, Edina, Minnesota 55439.

Library bound edition distributed by Rockbottom Books, Pentagon Tower, P.O. Box 36036, Minneapolis, Minnesota 55435.

Edited by: Rosemary Wallner

LIBRARY OF CONGRESS CATALOGING-IN-PUBLICATION DATA

Nielsen, Shelly, 1958-
    Thanksgiving / written by Shelly Nielsen; [edited by Rosemary Wallner]
    p. cm. -- (Holiday celebrations)
    Summary: Rhyming text introduces aspects of this important national holiday.
    ISBN 1-56239-068-6
    1. Thanksgiving Day--Juvenile literature. [1. Thanksgiving Day.] I. Wallner, Rosemary, 1964- II. Title. III.
Series: Nielsen, Shelly, 1958- Holiday celebrations.
GT4975.N54   1992   394.2'683--dc20   91-73033

International Standard Book Number:	Library of Congress Catalog Card Number:
1-56239-068-6	91-73033

marie.claude manchau

Celebrating
Thanksgiving

Dress-Up Day

The week before Thanksgiving,
Mrs. Hudson brought a box.
It was full to the brim
with clothes to dress in:
    capes and boots and socks.
We pretended we were settlers,
and it made us laugh and grin
when we looked in the mirror
wearing our bonnets and beards
    and saw real, live pilgrims!

Sail Away, Mayflower

Rock this way,
rock that way,
rock to and fro.
Sail away, pilgrims, on a great big boat.
You're going to America, your brand new home
with all your belongings stored below.
Rock this way,
rock that way,
rock to and fro.
Sail away, Mayflower, strong and slow.

Indian Friends

Here come Indians
to say hello.
  "Welcome, strangers,
  are you hungry and cold?
  Have some delicious bread to eat,
  and wear these moccasins on your feet.
  All winter we'll keep you safe from harm
  and give you blankets to keep you warm.
  From now on we'll do all we can
  to be your helpful, loyal friends."

Trace-A-Turkey

Want to trace a turkey?
It's easy as can be.
Just press your hand
on paper and draw
one-two-three . . .
Five fingers make feathers,
and black crayon makes a beak.
Add colorful feathers. There!
Your turkey is complete.

To Grandma's House

We're going to Grandma's
to see what's cooking in the oven.
We're going to Grandma's
to play with my cousins.
We're going to Grandma's
for a hug and some Thanksgiving loving.

Kitchen Helper

Let me help make dinner, please.
Though I may be small
I can do a lot of things
with hardly any help at all.
I can —

      peel the carrots,
      wash the peas,
      scrub the potatoes,
      stir the gravy.

And best of all,
if you wish,
I'll be a taster
of every dish.
      Mmm! Delish!

My Centerpiece

It's called a horn of plenty
but it's not meant to blow.
You put it on the table
and arrange it just so.
Fill it up with speckled maze
and gourds of orange and yellow.
But sometimes
I wear it as a funny hat.
    What a silly fellow!

Thanks!

I'm thankful for —
        Mom and Dad
        my punching bag
        fluffy clouds
        and stories read out loud,
mud cakes
creepy snakes
burps
and cricket chirps,
        slippery sledding hills
        twirls on carousels
        Saturday cartoons
        balloons
        Daddy's snores
        and toy stores.
Those are just
a few things
I am thankful for.

Finally — Dinnertime!

Pass the rolls,
brown and warm.
Pass the potatoes,
pass the corn.
Pass the carrots,
pass the peas
And don't forget
the wriggly cranberries.

Whew! I'm stuffed!
But I can't pass by
a giant slice of pumpkin pie.

Splash Happy

Time to do dishes!
I'll help, of course.
There's a pile of plates,
a heap of forks.
Aunt Tess washes
and I rub dry.
Grandma puts everything away.
When I gave my aunt
a little splash,
she didn't get mad —
she just splashed me back.

Pretend Turkey

Daddy, Daddy —
look at me.
Gobble! Gobble!
Who can I be?

   Look at my feathers.
   Look at my beak.
   Watch me peck grain to eat.

Did you guess yet?
Can't you see?
I'm a fat Thanksgiving turkey!

Yard Football!

Forty-nine . . . twenty-two . . . thirty-eight . . . hike!

Fullback,
Quarterback
    Run, run, run.
Look out!
Dodge about!
    Tackle to the ground.
Leap up,
take a whack.
    Isn't this fun?
Scream, shout.
Jump about.
    Hooray! Our team won!

marie claude blanchard

It's a Parade!

Far away,
a band starts to play.
The parade is marching through town!
Hear the drummers drumming?
The floats are coming
with flowers, balloons, and clowns.

Later today,
we'll be our own parade —
but we'll need a horn to blow,
plus a make-believe drum
and a song to hum.
Ready? Let's go!

Eating . . . Again?

Daddy said,
"Let's make leftovers,"
and he showed me how to do it.
Take bread and tomato,
turkey and mayo,
put a sandwich together, and chew it!
    Oh, yeah . . .
    I almost forgot:
    a glass of milk
    really hits the spot.